Remembering
Fort Wayne

Scott M. Bushnell

TURNER
PUBLISHING COMPANY

An emotional crowd gathers in the Allen County Courthouse in November 1942 to see the names of loved ones and friends as the Honor Roll of area servicemen and women is unveiled.

Remembering
Fort Wayne

Turner Publishing Company
www.turnerpublishing.com

Remembering Fort Wayne

Library of Congress Control Number: 2010924303

ISBN: 978-1-59652-649-5

Printed in the United States of America

ISBN 978-1-68336-831-1 (pbk.)

CONTENTS

A group of Fort Wayne fire fighters pose alongside one of a dozen fire trucks they built between 1938 and 1942. They bought the chassis and engine from International Harvester and used their skills to fabricate and assemble everything from the seat to the rear bumper.

ACKNOWLEDGMENTS

This volume, *Remembering Fort Wayne,* is the result of the cooperation and efforts of many individuals and organizations. It is with great thanks that we acknowledge the valuable contribution of the Allen County Public Library, the Allen County–Fort Wayne Historical Society, the Embassy Theatre Foundation, and the Library of Congress for their generous support.

We would also like to thank the following individuals for valuable contributions and generous assistance in making this work possible: Curt B. Witcher and John Beatty of the Allen County Public Library; Walter Font, curator, and Randy Elliott, collections assistant, of the Allen County–Fort Wayne Historical Society; Tom Castaldi of the Wabash & Erie Canal Society; Sam Hyde and Tasha Bushnell of Hyde Brothers Books, Fort Wayne; Donald Weber of the Fort Wayne Firefighters' Museum; Michael Patterson of Frost Illustrated; Steven Cox and David Latta of Turner Publishing; and especially Barbara W. Bushnell.

The goal in publishing this work is to provide broader access to a set of extraordinary photographs. The aim is to inspire, provide perspective, and evoke insight that might assist officials and citizens, who together are responsible for determining Fort Wayne's future. In addition, the book seeks to preserve the past with respect and reverence.

With the exception of cropping images where needed and touching up imperfections that have accrued over time, no other changes have been made. The caliber and clarity of many photographs are limited by the technology of the day and the ability of the photographer at the time they were made.

We encourage readers to reflect as they explore Fort Wayne, stroll along its streets, or wander its neighborhoods. It is the publisher's hope that in making use of this work, longtime residents will learn something new and that new residents will gain a perspective on where Fort Wayne has been, so that each can contribute to its future.

—*Todd Bottorff, Publisher*

PREFACE

The area known as Fort Wayne, Indiana, was a thriving center of commerce for hundreds of years before European trappers, traders, and settlers "discovered" it. It was formed by two rivers—the St. Mary's from the south and the St. Joseph from the northeast—that seem to meander over great distances before coming together to become the Maumee River and its run to Lake Erie. These waterways enabled Native Americans to bring pelts, food, tools, and crafts to the convergence of the rivers from as far away as what would later become Wisconsin and western New York. Furthermore, a short portage led to the Wabash River, which could carry a canoe to the Ohio and Mississippi rivers. To the Miami peoples who controlled what they called "Kekionga," the area where the Maumee formed was a glorious gateway.

There are three themes that resound throughout Fort Wayne's history. Commerce and transportation are two of them. Although the earliest settlers were attracted by the area's great groves of hardwood trees and arable land to grow crops, subsequent generations saw the promise of greater prosperity through the building of a canal to provide access for the Midwest to the Great Lakes and the Atlantic seaboard. In an engineering feat of almost heroic proportions, the Wabash & Erie Canal was carved through Ohio and Indiana, with the first boats traveling between Fort Wayne and Huntington in 1835. The boatloads of commodities and workers in the next few years swelled Fort Wayne from a town to a small city by 1840.

The building of the canal through swamp and wilderness exemplifies the third theme in Fort Wayne's history: the persistence of engineers, inventors, and businessmen to recognize opportunities and bring new products to the marketplace. The canal was replaced by the railroads, which built roundhouses, locomotive shops, and repair facilities as well as freight yards and depots. The city's economic growth, particularly in heavy manufacturing, was sustained by the railroads for six decades. In the 1920s, Fort Wayne convinced International Harvester to build its new truck plant here, creating thousands of manufacturing and support-industry jobs.

Fort Wayne's inventiveness wasn't limited to transportation. Men and women with vision played key roles in the community and industry: whether it was Henry Paul and John Peters manufacturing the first contained washing machine; or Theodore Thieme daring to bring a state-of-the-art knitting mill—machinery and manpower—from Germany to Fort Wayne; or Samuel Foster recognizing the opportunity in designing a blouse for women that became the fashionable style of the Gibson Girl; or Philo Farnsworth pioneering the development of television. Success wasn't the product of leadership alone; the highly skilled workers of the area also attracted a number of industries that grew up in Fort Wayne, particularly the magnet wire industry and related products that form the basis for modern electrical technology.

The economic downturn in heavy manufacturing had an effect on Fort Wayne in the latter half of the twentieth century. The demise of the railroads was a heavy blow and the north-south interstate highway that swept through the city did not create the immediate economic growth that rail-based commerce had a century before. The inability of manufacturing to adapt their older facilities to new production methods put Fort Wayne in with the rest of the so-called Rust Belt in the Midwest. The steady, at times alarming, loss of manufacturing firms deprived the city not only of high-paying jobs, but also of some of its pride. Retail activity in the downtown area—whose history is a central portion of this book—moved to the city-like malls on the perimeter of Fort Wayne.

Today, both the private and public sectors of the area are devoted to fostering new avenues to economic growth. Elements of Fort Wayne's heritage can be found in several new paths being followed by entrepreneurs. Universities and venture capital firms are investing in start-up firms in the health-care field that will benefit the nation's aging population. The transportation industry is experiencing growth in inter-modal transportation with truck trailers mounted on rail cars. And the rivers are being reclaimed environmentally as residents value them for their beauty, not just their economic efficacy. It will be interesting to see how Fort Wayne of the early twenty-first century is portrayed a century from now in whatever form image-and-text works of the future take.

Dams, reservoirs, and aqueducts were all required for the operation of the Wabash and Erie Canal. This 75-foot-wide dam on the St. Joseph River created a reservoir that supplied a small feeder canal whose water lifted the boats through the Summit City. It also provided good fishing and some challenging experiences in small boats after the canal's heyday was past.

ON THE RIGHT TRACK

(1880–1889)

A full-time professional fire department was a necessity in late-nineteenth-century cities where fire often meant calamity. This photograph of Fort Wayne's first full-time paid fire fighters in 1882 shows the chief and crew with a steamer and hose-and-ladder wagon. The firehouse was located on the northeast corner of Court and Berry streets.

It was said that the late nineteenth century prompted an unofficial competition to see who could build a church with the tallest spire. Few could compete with St. Paul's Evangelical Lutheran Church, shown here in its Gothic splendor shortly after its 1889 dedication.

Any panorama of Fort Wayne in the final decade of the 1800s undoubtedly revealed a skyline of spires. Few were so remarkably recognizable as the twin steeples of St. Paul's Catholic Church.

Columbia Street was the center of commerce for Fort Wayne from the earliest days of the Wabash & Erie Canal. Named for Dana Columbia, a canal boat and hotel owner, the street was also known as "the Landing" for settlers, businessmen, and scalawags. As can be seen, Columbia Street was still focused on the agricultural market half a century after its founding.

The Randall Hotel was among the most recognizable landmarks in all of Fort Wayne. Located on Harrison Street where Columbia Street ends, the building was a three-story granary and tannery when it was built in 1856. Remodeled and expanded, it became "the best $2 hotel in Indiana," attracting patrons like Buffalo Bill Cody.

This photograph of Calhoun Street is from Main Street, facing north, and shows the successful retail clothing businesses on the left and a trolley plying the thoroughfare. The Eckart & McCullochs block—as large buildings were called in those days—is visible on the left.

With its pilasters and pediment, Max L. Frankenstein's building on the northwest corner of Barr and Washington Street in the 1880s was a classic example of Victorian Renaissance architecture that was dominant in the Midwest. Frankenstein operated this store into the 1890s.

Built in 1863, the Aveline House quickly became known as one of the region's finest hotels. Facing the courthouse at Berry and Calhoun, it served well-to-do travelers, political candidates, and even local businessmen who wanted a prestigious address. Shown here in 1889 before a fifth story was added, the Aveline would become the scene of a tragic fire in 1908.

The Allen County Courthouse was feeling its age in 1889 when this photograph was taken. When it was dedicated in 1861, this—the third courthouse in the city's history—was said to be "designed to last a century." Less than 40 years later, its lack of modern amenities, such as workable plumbing, led city fathers to plan a new courthouse.

Frederick Eckart operated a meat market and pork packer near the center of the city before moving it to this location at West Main and Harrison streets.

Calhoun Street in the early 1890s offered a variety of stores, from Kuttner's on the left where suits were made to order, to Skelton, Watt and Wilt on the right, a wholesale grocer whose windows featured stylish shades. This view faces north from Jefferson Street.

Prevalent Prosperity

(1890–1915)

Calhoun got busier as one walked closer to the center of the community. This view in the early 1890s is from Wayne Street, facing north, toward more commercial activity. The five-story building at right is the Bass Block, and beyond it are the Aveline House and the trees in the courthouse yard.

The Reformed Church Orphans Home—officially known as Reformirtes Waifenhaus by the two German Reformed Church parishes that sponsored it—was built in 1894 on Lake Avenue to care for unwanted children. During the Great Depression, it took in not only orphans, but also children whose families could not care for them.

Located on Cass Street near the depot for the Lake Shore and Michigan Southern Railroad, this hotel was advertised as having "a first class bar and lunch room." One has to wonder how well its patrons could sleep, given its proximity to the tracks that can be seen in the lower right-hand portion of the photograph.

Dedicated in 1893 shortly before this photograph was taken, City Hall at Berry and Barr streets housed the Fort Wayne Police Department in addition to the offices of the mayor and the clerk as well as the municipal court. The police used this horse-drawn wagon to transport men and women to the jail that was in the City Hall basement.

The Barr Street Market assumed its pivotal role in the daily life of Fort Wayne when it was created in the 1840s by Samuel Hanna to provide residents of the then-young community with access to fresh produce. In this 1893 photograph, the market is alive with horses and wagons.

Every photograph tells a story and there certainly must be one about why these two conductors from the Fort Wayne Electric Railway Company have a donkey standing with them. Perhaps the donkey was saved by the "cowcatcher" on the front of the trolley. Or perhaps the merits of animal power versus electric power were under review.

The employees of Mayflower Mills were photographed at the rear of their building on Columbia Street in 1895. The bookkeepers and secretary are identifiable by their dresses; the teamsters by their stance near their horses; the mill workers by the amount of flour on their clothes; and the foreman by the jaunty angle of his hat. The fellow looking down from the roof is an unknown quantity.

Sylvanus F. Bowser was an inventor, industrialist, and philanthropist who revolutionized the oil and gas industry by inventing the self-measuring pump. He is standing at left in this 1890s photograph of his factory on East Creighton Avenue, watching over production. To Bowser's left, a little girl tends to a woman in a wheelchair.

Fort Wayne's centennial celebration was filled with parades, exhibits, and dances. The crowd outside the old Pennsylvania Railroad station seems to be waiting for the next round of activities.

Even the city's larger structures were decorated for the 1895 celebration, including the Pixley-Long building at 116-118 Berry Street. The building housed more than the popular People's Store. Upstairs were the offices of architects Wing and Mahurin, temperance publisher Mason Long, attorneys Ninde and Ninde, and real estate developer Louis Curdes. All played pivotal roles in Fort Wayne's history.

The new brick Wayne Street Methodist Episcopal Church was built in 1871 at Wayne and Broadway.
It was remodeled and enlarged 25 years later.

The growing prosperity and culture of Fort Wayne can be seen in this 1898 photograph looking north on Calhoun Street from Washington. Not only are the streets paved, but there are competing piano stores on opposite corners. Farther down the left side of Calhoun, there are offices of dentists, insurance salesmen, and architects.

Lakeside was one of Fort Wayne's attractive new neighborhoods in the 1890s. Located northeast of the city's center and north of the Maumee River, the neighborhood was served by the Lakeside School on Rivermet Avenue at Oneida Street from 1896 to 1959.

The White National Bank was formed in 1892 by businessman and former Congressman John B. White. Located at Wayne and Clinton streets, the bank survived the 1893 financial panic before being consolidated with the First National Bank in 1905.

Fort Wayne was in step with the national cycling craze in the 1890s. These young men are posing in Swinney Park with the top of the park pavilion visible in the background.

The parlor recreation of singing along with a pianist began to be supplanted in the late nineteenth century with that of formal listening. Three young men seem hypnotized as they listen intently to a recording played on a Victor Talking Machine Company Gramophone in July 1900.

One of the most popular brands of cigar was the "Pony," manufactured by George R. Reiter, who is shown here in his store at Barr and Berry streets in the early 1900s. Reiter is at far-left, with his wife Mary Ann Payne beside him. The empty chair and strategically placed spittoon suggest they expected the photographer to sit down and talk for a spell.

There was significant cultural pride among the German-speaking immigrants who helped Fort Wayne prosper in the nineteenth century. Singing societies, athletic competitions, and literary and political groups flourished within the immigrant community. In the decades before World War I, even young boys fancied themselves soldiering in their ancestors' armies.

Fort Wayne built its ballpark on the "flats" where downtown met the St. Mary's River, and scenes like this March 1904 flood were common for decades. The Fort Wayne Railroaders team in the Central League was forced to relocate to Canton, Ohio, in mid-season by the flood damage.

Built in 1895 at Calhoun and Wayne streets, the International Order of Odd Fellows building featured a distinctive and dominating design. The Fort Wayne Commercial Club, the forerunner of the Chamber of Commerce, was located here as well as one of the city's fine jewelers, August Bruder. The intersection's arc light and its gas-fueled or kerosene-fueled lamp on the corner are both visible in this 1905 image.

The Federal Building and Post Office was located at Berry and Clinton streets. Completed in 1899, the building resembled the Fort Wayne City Hall in size and design. It would be demolished in 1938.

Although their hats may not be identical, the burden distributed among the mail carriers was consistent. This is a normal workload for Fort Wayne postmen at a time when 54 mail trains stopped daily and 4 deliveries a day were required to downtown addresses.

The 28th annual Grand Army of the Republic encampment brought thousands of people to Fort Wayne to see the Union Army veterans on parade in May 1907. The grand arch in front of the Elektron Building on Berry Street carried the images of three Civil War hometown heroes: Sion Bass, Henry Lawton, and Charles Zollinger.

On the day after the Aveline Hotel fire, small crowds gathered to view the charred remains as workmen sifted through the rubble for victims. Great piles of debris covered the street. Luggage, clothing, and jewelry were uncovered and taken to the courthouse for identification. While the fire raged through the Aveline, it apparently did little damage to the more modern Pixley-Long building.

37

The Charles Crawford family is resplendent in their shiny automobile and finest outerwear in this 1908 image.

A copy of Brentwood Tolan's architectural drawings for the Allen County Courthouse resides in the Louvre, where it is valued as an example of early-twentieth-century U.S. architecture. Dedicated in 1902, the courthouse is a national treasure with its exterior sculpture and interior murals. When this photograph was taken in 1909, it dominated the city skyline. In the foreground, a new building finally rises from the ashes of the Aveline Hotel.

The two-story building to the right of the baggage platform is the Pennsylvania Railroad Station that served Fort Wayne prior to 1914. This is the station where Abraham Lincoln changed trains in the early morning hours of February 23, 1860, en route to New York City for his famous speech at Cooper Union.

Smoke billows from the Mayflower Mills building on Columbia Street between Harrison and Calhoun on May 21, 1911. Although it appears the police have roped off the area, at least one pedestrian passing Fisher Brothers Paper at left seems to be wholly uninterested in approaching the fire for a closer look.

The worst train wreck within Fort Wayne city limits occurred on August 13, 1911, when a speeding Pennsylvania Railroad passenger train crashed into a freight train in Swinney Park. Three railroad men were killed and 35 passengers and crew were injured. The crash, which resulted from the passenger train trying to make up lost time, attracted hundreds to the scene.

Miss Betty McCulloch, seated in the rocking chair, celebrated her birthday on September 5, 1911, with a special party at her "cottage" at 376 E. Berry Street. Among her friends in attendance was Jane Alice Peters, sixth child from the left, seated on the stoop. Miss Peters would be hailed two decades later as one of Hollywood's greatest actresses, Carole Lombard.

Mayor William Hosey championed the elevation of the railroad beds through the city when he took office in 1909, arguing that the trains snarled traffic and impeded the city's growth. Although he succeeded in fashioning a plan for the Pennsylvania and Wabash railroads to raise their trackbeds—as shown here in 1911 near the Weber Hotel at 1601 S. Calhoun Street—the city would not realize a midtown elevation until the 1950s.

Depending on one's perspective, the Wigwam Saloon was on the right—or wrong—side of the tracks.
The Wigwam served Fort Wayne's Centlivre Special beer, which undoubtedly met the approval of
those who frequented the tavern, located right next to the railroad tracks.

The General Electric plant in Fort Wayne was ahead of its time with an on-the-job training program for employees. A course included blueprint reading, mathematics, and other subjects related to the employees' tasks in the shop.

The massive flood in March 1913 devastated much of the Midwest, leaving neighborhoods and even whole communities isolated. The daily newspaper was often the sole source of news, which is why the *Journal-Gazette* sent its horse-drawn delivery wagons through axle-deep water to get its extra editions into the hands of its readers during the crisis.

Art Smith captured the hearts and imaginations of people around the world in 1915 with his daredevil feats in the air. The self-taught aviator from Fort Wayne thrilled crowds with loop-to-loops and nighttime skywriting using phosphorous candles. He even won the hearts of some romantics by eloping with his sweetheart, Aimee, in his biplane.

Henry Hilbrecht was instrumental in building the fire department into a professional force. He became the city's first full-time paid fireman in 1873 and its first official fire chief in 1873. He scrapped old equipment, built five firehouses, and replaced cisterns with hydrants. Hilbrecht also had his own car—in this case, a new 1912 Speedwell—which he and his grandson are enjoying here.

Although Fort Wayne has a proud history in Organized Baseball, its industrial or semi-professional leagues provided some of the most affordable, exciting entertainment. The men pictured here not only played for the Rolling Mill team, they also held down strenuous jobs at the mill.

The nation's symbol of independence traveled from Philadelphia to San Francisco in 1915, and one of its stops was in Fort Wayne on July 6. The event was held at the new Pennsylvania Railroad station, where more than 50,000 people viewed the Liberty Bell.

The Indiana Horticultural Society placed a marker at Swinney Park in 1916 to memorialize the work of John Chapman, better known as Johnny Appleseed. Chapman spent the last 10 years of his life tending to thousands of trees he had planted east of Fort Wayne along the Maumee River. Chapman died in 1845 and the society's marker is believed to be near where he was buried.

GROWTH AND GRIT

(1916–1940)

The founders of the Y.W.C.A. in Fort Wayne were honored with a "Pioneer Days" celebration in 1916. The Y.W.C.A. had built a "safe home" for young working women on West Wayne in 1913 and added an annex six years later.

E. C. Rurode was one of Fort Wayne's leading retailers in the late nineteenth and early twentieth centuries with his New York Store on Calhoun Street across from the courthouse. In his youth he was one of the founding members of the first professional baseball team in the city and throughout his life a bit of a dandy, as this photograph suggests.

The funeral procession for Assistant Fire Chief George W. Jasper in March 1917 included a delegation of Fort Wayne police marching in the rain.

The renowned Packard Piano and Organ Company changed its tune in World War I, carefully crafting airplane propellers for the army in its Fort Wayne plant. The answer to the sign hung from the ceiling (asking "Who's the Boss?") seems to be clear when one looks at the foreman overseeing the workers.

By 1918, there was a shortage of food supplies because of the war, and shoppers had to use a 50-50 rule when buying scarce commodities such as sugar and flour. Under the government plan, for example, one could buy five pounds of sugar only if he or she were also buying five pounds of a substitute for sugar.

Red Cross fund-raising activities in Fort Wayne during World War I included selling roses at the 1918 Liberty Gardens Fair.

Every part of American society was asked to do its share in World War I. Here the Lincoln School Canning Club shows its contribution to the war effort in 1918.

Fort Wayne responded the same as every other American city when the armistice was declared on November 11, 1918—with spontaneous bell-ringing, parades, and cheering. Some found unusual ways to make noise, like the woman on the rear of the vehicle banging the inside of her cooking pot with a hammer.

The Allen County and Fort Wayne Memorial to World War I was dedicated in 1920. With a
doughboy on one side and a sailor on the other, the monument in Memorial Park lists those who died
in the war.

The return to prosperous times after World War I led to greater demands on public services. The back-breaking work of tearing up and repaving Calhoun Street south of Main Street was captured in this June 30, 1929, image.

Theodore Thieme, at center in the front row with the white suit and dark tie, founded Wayne Knitting Mills in 1891. Thieme was a generous industrialist, trying to provide what he felt was right for his workers. Among his efforts was this annual outing at his home for longtime employees.

Fort Wayne continued to be a railroad hub into the early twentieth century. Few connections were as easy as when passengers could cross from the Wabash Railway depot, on the right, to the Pennsylvania Railroad station, at left in the distance.

The Wayne Hotel was the first 100-room hotel in the city when it was built on Columbia Street in 1887. Still prospering in the 1920s, the hotel was located on the site of the original Dana Columbia house. It continued to operate until a February 1975 fire led to its demolition.

A sea of students at South Side High School demonstrates synchronized exercises at a field day in the 1920s. The school was built in 1922.

North Side High School was completed on State Boulevard in 1927 near the St. Joseph River. It was one of the city's first $1 million projects.

This vehicle was among the first of more than a million trucks produced at the International Harvester plant. Fort Wayne's success at outbidding 26 other cities for the truck manufacturer became one of its greatest commercial triumphs in the twentieth century.

It is opening night in May 1928 for the Emboyd, a movie palace and vaudeville house on Jefferson Boulevard. Over the years the Emboyd featured stars of stage and screen, including Bob Hope whose first emcee job was there. In 1952, its name was changed to the Embassy. Twenty years later, a handful of community volunteers saved it from demolition and it stands today as the last of the majestic theaters in Fort Wayne.

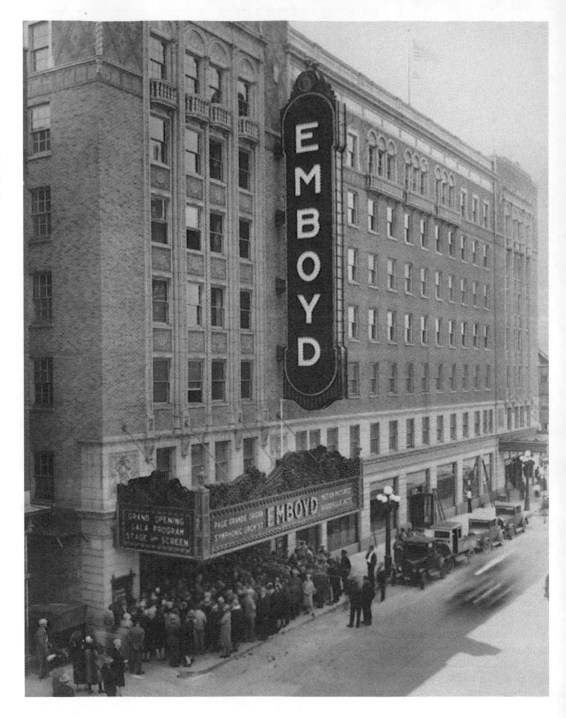

The Public Library began an outreach program to disadvantaged children in 1927 with a "book wagon," bringing reading material to kids on summer vacation. This visit occurred near the Rolling Mill School, which served the area around the Fort Wayne Iron and Steel plant off Taylor Street.

The Bowser certified measurable gasoline pumps are prominently displayed at the Penn-Marr Petroleum gas station at Packard and Fairfield in this 1927 photograph. Walter Warriner was the proprietor of this station.

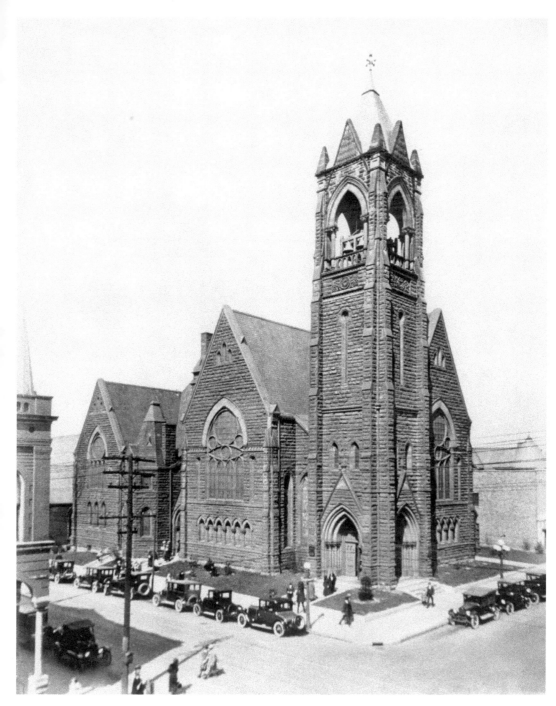

It appears that this 1920s photograph of the First Presbyterian Church located at Clinton and Washington streets was taken on a busy Sunday as parishioners headed to church.

The Fort Wayne Public Library was built in 1904 with the help of a $90,000 grant from Andrew Carnegie's philanthropic foundation. The Greek Revival structure, built from buff-colored Indiana Bedford limestone, would be razed in 1965.

The South Wayne School was built in the 1890s and continued to serve its neighborhood until being replaced in 1962. This photograph of a reading class was recorded around 1928.

There were plenty of high hopes when Board Chairman Sam Foster broke ground for the Lincoln Bank Tower in August 1929. A little more than a month later, the stock market collapsed. Fort Wayne's first skyscraper was completed in 1930, and Lincoln Bank was one of two banks in the city to survive President Roosevelt's bank holiday without undergoing a reorganization.

The Achduth Vesholom congregation was formed in 1848, and this synagogue at Wayne and Fairfield streets served as its home from 1916 to 1958.

Fort Wayne was among the many U.S. cities vying for airmail service in 1930 and managed to send more than 45,000 letters the first day of service. George Hill was the pilot in the first flight, shown here in the cockpit of his biplane at Smith Field. In April 1932, Hill was killed when his plane crashed on a Fort Wayne–to–South Bend flight.

Two baseball players pose at key points in their careers at League Park in 1931. Playing for the Lady Wayne Chocolates, a semi-pro team, were Earl Bolyard, left, and Everett Scott. Bolyard was about to embark on his minor league career while Scott had retired from the Major Leagues where he was known as the "iron man." Scott had played in 1,307 consecutive games from 1916 to 1925 with the Boston Red Sox and New York Yankees.

This 1930s photograph was taken after city firemen had restored the department's 1848 Button Hand Pumper. The pumper, which arrived in the city by way of the Wabash & Erie Canal, required six men on each side to operate it and send water through leather hose, which was riveted together. The Button is now in the Firefighters Museum in Fort Wayne.

Built in 1893, Fort Wayne's Victorian-era City Hall was beginning to show wear in the 1930s. Its sandstone was beginning to darken from the accumulated soot from coal-fired locomotives and coal-heated homes. Also visible in this image are the Barr Street Market on the right and the City Utilities Building to the left of City Hall.

Where once there had been horses and wagons, now there were cars and trucks. Market day on Barr Street was a time of congestion—equally so early in the twentieth century and here, in the 1930s.

The lobby and main stairs of the Fort Wayne Public Library was the ideal place to assemble if one were a child wanting to attend the Story Hour in the 301 West Wayne Street building.

The new Pennsylvania Lines depot—more commonly known as the Baker Street Station—was built in 1914 to serve the growing demand for rail passenger service. Before World War I, Pennsy service through Fort Wayne included ten trains to Chicago and ten more to the East every day.

This close-up of the main building of the Three Rivers Filtration and Pumping Station more closely resembles a castle than a public utility. The water treatment facility was part of a $2.5 million project in 1930 that also included a dam on the St. Joseph River and a reservoir.

The Hoagland School was opened in the year the Civil War ended, but it was still operating when this 1930s photograph was taken. The school was located on the northeast corner of Hoagland and Butler streets.

The Lincoln Bank Tower changed the Fort Wayne skyline, as this image facing south along Calhoun Street demonstrates. The crossing tower, used to lower and raise gates across the street, was a common sight where busy rails and streets converged.

This well-crafted wagon, powered by a real horse, was a rarity on city streets in the late 1920s. As the Great Depression wore on however, scenes like this one became more common.

This Barr Street building was once the bustling home of the Kunkle Valve Works, a company renowned for its critical safety equipment that kept boilers, engines, and pipelines from exploding. When this photograph was taken in January 1939, it housed a far different company—Martin Wrecking.

The Phyllis Wheatley Social Center on East Douglas Street became the most important agency for African-Americans in Fort Wayne in the 1920s, offering a variety of programs. In 1936, for example, recreation and reading programs were offered at its Westfield Community Center on Taylor Street. The Wheatley Center became Fort Wayne's Urban League a decade later.

Indiana University opened its first Fort Wayne Extension Center in 1917 to offer classes in the community. This Barr Street building served as its home after 1939 until Indiana and Purdue universities combined their local classes.

Mayor Harry Baals, center, was on hand to greet orchestra leader Paul Whiteman at the railroad station in February 1939. Whiteman and his renowned jazz orchestra played a three-night stand at the Paramount.

The family-owned Centlivre Brewery was a key part of Fort Wayne from its inception in 1862. It gained renown with its Nickel Plate Beer, the exclusive beer served on the Nickel Plate Railroad. This building on the St. Joseph River was crowned with a statue of the founder, Charles Louis Centlivre.

The Anthony Hotel, built in 1908, reigned as the grand hotel in Fort Wayne for decades. The 9-story, 263-room hotel was the city's finest meeting place and convention center as evidenced by this image of its mezzanine and the ballroom entrance.

Victory's Engine

(1941–1950s)

The Grand Leader Department Store reigned supreme from its location on the southeast corner of Wayne and Calhoun streets. This had been the scene of one of the great fires in downtown Fort Wayne when a December 1927 blaze gutted the Grand Leader. A year later, the building shown here was erected.

The economic recovery is evidenced here by the number of automobiles in the downtown retail area. Another indicator was Wolf & Dessauer, seen on the left in this photograph of Washington and Calhoun, proudly advertising in 1941 that it was fully air-conditioned.

This is a rare view from the roof of City Hall on Berry Street in November 1941. Recorded by Ellsworth Crick, it is the skyline to the west, using infrared film. The blurred figure at right is one of the roof ornaments.

Most Precious Blood Catholic Church opened its school in 1929 at Barthold and Spring streets. Despite a difficult beginning in the Depression, the school prospered in the 1940s, as seen here, and into the next century.

Patriotism was evident everywhere at the start of the war. The American Legion Post's 40 & 8 "Black Jack" engine was a frequent parade participant. The 40 & 8 is a fraternal organization honoring U.S. veterans of World War I in France. The Fort Wayne chapter obtained permission from General John Pershing's family to use the general's nickname for their engine.

The Auto-Inn Garage on West Washington Boulevard owned by Ambrose Hayes and Raymond Young supported the war effort by gladly taking all donations as the city's "scrap rubber depot" in June 1942.

More than $650,000 was raised in the literary bond drive at the public library in October 1943. Lincoln Life paid $20,000 for Carl Van Doren's notated copy of *The Secret History of the American Revolution* and then donated the book to the library.

Nothing went to waste in the war effort. Even fat from cooking could be used in making war materiel. Here a Brownie and a Girl Scout bring the waste fats they have collected from homes in their neighborhood and turn them over at Samuel Manning's meat store on West Foster Parkway.

Shoppers standing outside the Morris Lunch Room look for their northbound streetcar on Calhoun Street near Washington in this late February 1945 photograph.

There are more women in the wartime workforce and electric-powered buses are replacing streetcars in this March 1945 image outside the General Electric complex on Broadway. Records show that trolleys and streetcars carried 36.2 million riders in Fort Wayne in 1944.

Mayor Harry Baals, center, is obviously pleased that this June 1944 War Bond drive has raised $1 million. Flanking the mayor are Major Walker Bud Mahurin of Fort Wayne, then America's top war ace, and Lieutenant Charles Hall, the first pilot among the Tuskegee Airmen to shoot down three Nazi fighter planes, who was visiting family in Fort Wayne.

Life began to return to normal in late 1945, even to the extent that the National Peanut Company store on Calhoun Street went to great heights to help promote Fire Prevention Week. Fireman Ralph Fredericks steadies the store's Mr. Peanut on the ladder.

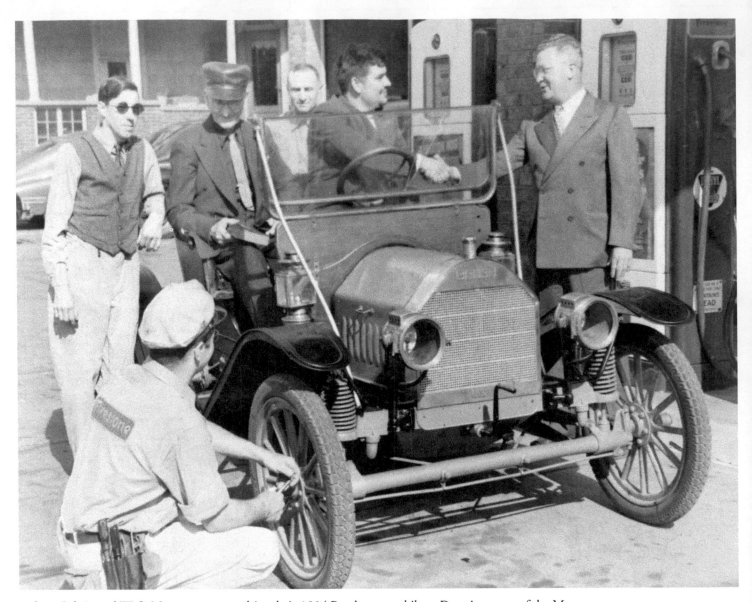

Robert Gehrig and W. S. Mason prepare to drive their 1904 Brush automobile to Detroit as part of the May 1946 Automotive Industries Golden Jubilee Celebration. Their drive from the Firestone Garage at Fairfield and Jefferson in Fort Wayne to the Detroit city limits took eight hours: the Brush averaged 40 miles per gallon and ran on a one-cylinder engine and wooden axles.

President Harry Truman's whistlestop campaign to win re-election in 1948 included a brief visit to Fort Wayne at the Pennsylvania Railroad station. In this election and those throughout most of the twentieth century, Fort Wayne voters favored the Republican candidate for president.

G. C. Murphy's at Wayne and Calhoun was a shining light in the retail sector of downtown Fort Wayne. Its bright limestone structure replaced the heavy brownstone IOOF Building at Wayne and Calhoun in October 1950.

Fort Wayne was among the first cities to implement an emergency fire telephone number. The "119" number was promoted throughout the city in 1950, with members of Junior Chamber of Commerce stenciling reminders on streetcorner sidewalks.

The Van Orman Hotel at Harrison and Berry streets was the new name of the refurbished Anthony Hotel. It was known in the early 1950s for its stylish New Coral Room with nightly dancing, and equally renowned for its 24-hour coffee shop on the corner.

Not so well known as Budweiser's Clydesdales, the show horses used by Berghoff Brewing to pull its beer barrel wagon were very popular in northern Indiana parades. Berghoff was first brewed in Fort Wayne in 1887.

Fort Wayne's John Oldham (no. 4) has already slipped past one future NBA Hall-of-Famer, Ed Macauley, as another at the far right, Bob Cousy, looks stunned in this game with the Boston Celtics during the 1950-51 season. The Zollner Pistons were an integral part of professional basketball before the team moved to Detroit in 1957.

Crossing a street in downtown Fort Wayne in the 1950s meant one had to look in both directions. But this group of pedestrians at Barr and Jefferson streets seems to be more interested in "You can see the difference" in the Arvin "Dual Power" TV advertised on the side of the bus than in oncoming traffic.

The Rialto Theater on South Calhoun showed more than its share of blockbuster movies, and for a time it had a future star on its staff. Marilyn Maxwell attended Central High School and worked as an usher in the 1930s at the Rialto before going on to a successful acting career.

International Harvester's truck manufacturing complex, shown here on June 12, 1951, had come a long way since its 1923 beginning. The company's one-millionth truck would roll off the line in 1973.

It's not a big sale at Wolf & Dessauer Department Store, but a fire drill in 1951. Fort Wayne had experienced more than its share of large fires in the downtown area over the years, prompting the Fire Department to conduct extensive safety campaigns.

The Fort Wayne Daisies were in "a league of their own" in 1952 when they were managed by Hall of Fame slugger Jimmy Foxx. The Daisies were the city's most admired sports team in the late 1940s and early 1950s before the All-America Girls Professional Baseball League folded.

The Allen County War Memorial Coliseum opened in what was then the outskirts of Fort Wayne, as this aerial photograph shows. The coliseum has hosted thousands of sporting events, carnivals, home and garden shows, and rock concerts.

When the Memorial Coliseum was dedicated in 1952, Bob Hope and Marilyn Maxwell were two of the stars saluting the community's newest entertainment facility. Hope was fond of Fort Wayne and remembered performing at the Embassy. Maxwell grew up in the city.

There has always been more than professional sports in Fort Wayne. This ball game at the old Municipal Beach Park is an example of the fun and recreation that has been part of Fort Wayne since its earliest days.

This southeasterly view from the courthouse stretches from the Lincoln Bank in the foreground to the white facade of Wolf & Dessauer's to the prominent steeple of St. Mary's Church and beyond.

The impact of other forms of transportation on the nation's railroads became increasingly evident in the 1950s. The old Wabash Railway depot became the Norfolk & Western Railroad station, but that didn't stop the railroad's legendary "Wabash Cannonball" from coming to the end of its line in May 1971.

The Fort Wayne Komets skated into the hearts of Fort Wayne fans when the Veterans Memorial Coliseum opened in 1952. Ever since then, its hard-nosed, championship play has attracted a loyal, vocal fan base, typifying what minor league hockey can achieve in a community.

The overhead wires so integral to public transportation were taking on a different dimension in the 1950s, when more people preferred to use their own cars. This photograph shows the electrified web along Calhoun Street from Main Street in the mid-1950s.

In 1958, the city demolished the Barr Street pavilion to make way for a parking lot. It was a poor ending for what had been the city's open air marketplace from its early days. Fifteen years later, volunteers would try to revive the market in a smaller space.

Wolf & Dessauer, which was founded in 1896, operated from this landmark building at Calhoun and Washington streets, on the right, from 1919 until 1959. The firm chose to build a new store downtown—at Wayne and Clinton streets—in the face of a growing trend of retail establishments moving to suburban shopping centers.

This photograph makes a different kind of statement about the changing nature of American cities, including Fort Wayne. Parked in front of the Allied Loan Company and the Royal Tavern on East Main Street is a foreign-made car, a Volkswagen "Beetle."

A December 29, 1958, fire in the MacDougal Building caused this tense moment as firemen give oxygen to an overcome colleague. The fire—one of several massive fires that winter—destroyed the 101-year-old building at Calhoun and Berry streets.

Fort Wayne's downtown profile as seen from the air, around 1960.

NOTES ON THE PHOTOGRAPHS

These notes, listed by page number, attempt to include all aspects known of the photographs. Each of the photographs is identified by the page number, a title or description, photographer and collection, archive, and call or box number when applicable. Although every attempt was made to collect all data, in some cases complete data may have been unavailable due to the age and condition of some of the photographs and records.

Printed in the USA
CPSIA information can be obtained
at www.ICGtesting.com
JSHW072024140824
68134JS00042B/3771